12/06

W9-BLU-110

The Inside Story
Log Cabin

Dana Meachen Rau

Marshall Cavendish Benchmark
New York

Boyle County Public Library

Inside a Log Cabin

1   chimney

2   door

3   loft

4   logs

5   notches

6   shingles

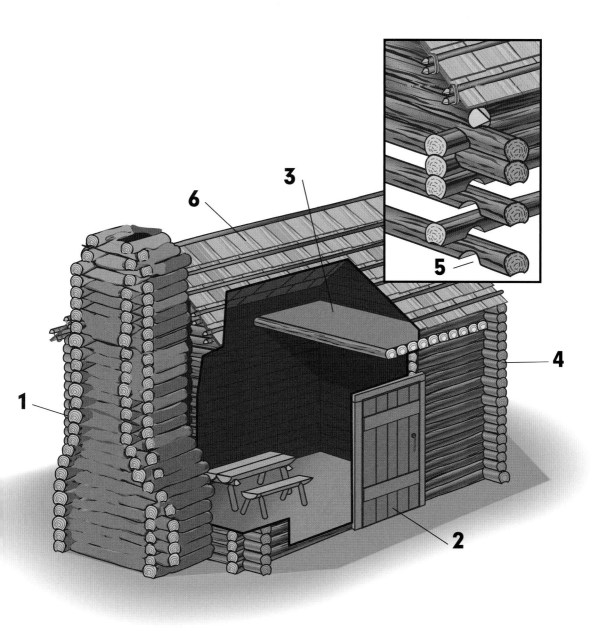

Long ago, there were many forests.

The forests were filled with trees.

People used the trees to make houses.

Log cabins were their homes.

Many people helped build a log cabin.

They brought their own tools.

They cut logs with axes and saws.

Horses pulled the logs.

They put long logs on each side.

They put shorter logs on each end.

They cut *notches* at the end of the logs.

Then they put more logs on top.

The walls grew taller.

They filled in cracks with stones and mud.

The roof was covered with *shingles*.

These were short boards split from logs.

They made a *chimney*.

They made it out of stone or hard mud.

They cut out a doorway.

They made a door out of wood.

Inside, the floor was dirt or wood.

They made tables and benches from wood, too.

Boyle County Public Library

The family cooked meals in the fireplace.

Log cabins were strong homes of wood.

Inside a Log Cabin

chimney

door

fireplace

notches

shingles

walls

Challenge Words

chimney (CHIM-nee) A pipe that carries smoke out of a building.

notches (NACH-is) Grooves in the logs that fit into each other.

shingles (SHIN-guhls) Short pieces of split wood.

Index

Page numbers in **boldface** are illustrations.

About the Author

Dana Meachen Rau is an author, editor, and illustrator. A graduate of Trinity College in Hartford, Connecticut, she has written more than one hundred fifty books for children, including nonfiction, biographies, early readers, and historical fiction. She lives with her family in Burlington, Connecticut.

Reading Consultants

Nanci Vargus, Ed.D. is an Assistant Professor of Elementary Education at the University of Indianapolis.

Beth Walker Gambro received her M.S. Ed. Reading from the University of St. Francis, Joliet, Illinois.

With thanks to Nanci Vargus, Ed.D. and
Beth Walker Gambro, reading consultants

Marshall Cavendish Benchmark
Marshall Cavendish
99 White Plains Road
Tarrytown, New York 10591-9001
www.marshallcavendish.us

Text copyright © 2007 by Marshall Cavendish Corporation

All rights reserved. No part of this book may be reproduced or utilized in any form or
by any means electronic or mechanical, including photocopying, recording, or by any information
storage and retrieval system, without written permission from the copyright holders.

Library of Congress Cataloging-in-Publication Data

Rau, Dana Meachen, 1971–
Log cabin / by Dana Meachen Rau.
p. cm. — (Bookworms, the inside story)
Includes index.
ISBN-13: 978-0-7614-2274-7
ISBN-10: 0-7614-2274-9
1. Log cabins—Juvenile literature. I. Title II. Series: Rau, Dana
Meachen, 1971- . Bookworks. Inside story.
NA8470.R38 2006
728.7'3—dc22
2005031261

Photo Research by Anne Burns Images

Cover Photo by Corbis/Richard T. Nowitz

The photographs in this book are used with permission and through the courtesy of:
Art Resource: pp. 1, 19, 29tl SEF. Corbis: p. 5 PBNJ Productions; p. 7 F. Damm/zefa;
p. 9 Vince Streano; p. 11 Raymond Gehman; p. 13 Joseph Sohm; pp. 15, 28br Jack Fields;
pp. 17, 29tr Lowell Georgia; pp. 21, 28tl Royalty-Free; pp. 23, 28tr Buddy Mays;
p. 25 Scott T. Smith; pp. 27, 28bl Robert Holmes.

Printed in Malaysia
1 3 5 6 4 2